SPRUNG

As we race through our two worlds, emailing and cell-phoning, David Madden's collection, *Sprung From The Soil*, beckons us to a time when Americans recognized their connection with nature and lived attuned to her rhythms and rigorous demands. Reading these poems reacquaints us with the physical work of growing, harvesting and preserving crops in order to eat and have medicinal remedies. We are reintroduced to the work of shearing, carding and spinning wool in order to make fabric that becomes warm clothing.

A world has been recreated in these poems ~ a world that helps us remember the intimate relationship our forebears had with earth, her creatures and seasons. In this collection, the late eighteenth and early nineteenth century inhabitants of Old Sturbridge Village walk through their quiet lives, adhering to their strict roles. Thus they show us how much we've left behind, yet how much we still depend on our connection with the land and each other in this continuing dance of life and death, here, on earth.

    Jude Rittenhouse
      Pablo Neruda Prize for Poetry finalist for 2003 and 2007
      Emily Dickinson Award honorable mention for 2002
      Living In Skin (Forest Song Press 2009)
      Westerly, RI

Each well-crafted poem in this collection sheds light on a piece of history. Here is Old Sturbridge Village as it was centuries ago~the people who built its houses, schools, and places of worship, tended its gardens and livestock, developed its commerce and guarded its finances. Just as these were a humble people, there is a gentle humility in these poems. A perfect collection for the student or teacher of history or for a parent to read aloud. Ian Newbury's illustrations make the perfect complement.

    Melanie Greenhouse
      Poet and playwright, Noank, CT

SPRUNG FROM THE SOIL

BEING

A SERIES OF POEMS ON
OLD STURBRIDGE VILLAGE

BY
DAVID JAMES MADDEN

WITH ILLUSTRATIONS
BY IAN NEWBURY

© COPYRIGHT 2009 GARDEN PATCH BOOKS

© COPYRIGHT 2009 GARDEN PATCH BOOKS

All Rights Reserved. No portion of this publication may be reproduced in any form or format without express written consent of the publisher.

ISBN: 978-0-9843119-0-3

Printed in the U.S.A

David James Madden: davidjamesmadden67@gmail.com

TABLE OF CONTENTS

Sprung from the Soil 3

CENTER VILLAGE

Barefoot Days 7
The Small House 8
An Herb Garden 10
The Quaker Meetinghouse 11
The Meetinghouse 12
The Burial Ground 14
The Fenno House 16
The Fitch House 18
The Thompson Bank 20
The Printing Office 22
The Cider Mill 23
The Salem Towne House 24
The Salem Towne Garden 26
The Bullard Tavern 27
The Tin Shop 28
The Parsonage 29
The John McClellan Law Office 30
The Asa Knight Store 31
The Village Common 32
The Shoe Shop 33
The Pound 34

Country Side

The District School 37
The Hervey Brooks Pottery Shop. 38
The Powder House. 39
The Pliny Freeman Farm 40
The Cooper's Shop 42
The Bixby House 44
The Blacksmith Shop. 45
The Dummerston Bridge. 46

Mill Neighborhood

The Carding Mill 51
The Grist Mill 52
The Saw Mill 54

To all who have made Old Sturbridge Village
a place of learning and enchantment
through the years.

The poems in this book are, for the most part, arranged in the same order one could take when seeing the different exhibits after leaving the Visitor's Center. An exception to this order is the book's placement of the Dummerston Bridge in the Countryside rather than after the Mill Neighborhood. Another exception is the placement in the book of The Powder House before arriving at the Pliny Freeman Farm. The Pasture Walk that leads to the Powder House begins at the Freeman Farm.

SPRUNG FROM THE SOIL

SPRUNG FROM THE SOIL

In ancient times, people held a belief
That a grasshopper didn't have a birth
But was formed directly within the earth
And came to life sprung from the soil.

So too now with this rural museum,
To teach us the history of our nation,
'Twas formed within the imagination
And came to life sprung from the soil.

CENTER VILLAGE

BAREFOOT DAYS

Most children go barefoot all summer long.
The one time a week they cover their feet
Is in church when they bring their shoes along
To slip them on before taking a seat.

And women too, when the weather is nice,
Are often unshod while doing their chores,
But when October foretells snow and ice,
All put on shoes before going outdoors.

THE SMALL HOUSE

Measuring twenty-one feet by twenty,
There's not much room for a family of five,
But in a village where some have plenty,
For others, it's a struggle to survive.
Those of African or native descent
Live in a different world than many whites.
Some are farmers who pay landowners rent,
They work just as hard, but not with the same rights,
Not when a man's judged by the color of his face.
An equal chance hasn't been given to all
When a hard-working man, due to his race,
Shelters his family in a house too small.

The Small House

AN HERB GARDEN

The capable wife knows what she needs
To keep her family safe from harm.
Her medicine grows from garden seeds
Found on every New England farm.
For coughs she uses thyme in tea,
Gives tarragon to soothe toothache,
Lavender serves as a remedy
When, instead of sleep, one lies awake.
And when she cooks, her family savors
The taste that marjoram lends to meat;
She knows full well how spearmint flavors
Jellies, syrup and a candy treat,
And how rosemary, cut in September,
Then can be used to help one remember.

THE QUAKER MEETINGHOUSE
1796

This meetinghouse has no steeple.
Its clapboard walls are plain and gray,
Not unlike the peculiar people
Who gather here in silence to pray.
Here they have neither clergy nor creed
Nor any religious ornament.
They seek each day in their word and deed
To be honest and benevolent.
They believe no one should be a slave
For each heart holds that of God within.
The Underground Railroad helps them save
Their fellow man from the nation's sin.

THE MEETINGHOUSE
1832

Standing at the head of the green,
Its steeple reaching to the sky,
The meetinghouse, tall and serene,
Greets all villagers passing by.

Inside its walls, each rented pew,
With door to keep out dogs and draft,
Is furnished by the well-to-do
With footrests and such other craft.

Folk gather on the Sabbath to pray
And to hear the minister preach.
Meetings last just about all day,
Morning, afternoon, two hours each.

This is the place voters elect
State officials and decide tax rates.
Here, every four years, men select
The man to lead the United States.

The Meetinghouse

THE BURIAL GROUND

There is, in the village burial ground,
A plot with a recently set headstone
Near where earth is piled in a tiny mound.
Here lies, beneath flowers lovingly grown,

The daughter of Hazen and Martha Horne.
They gave her the name Elizabeth Anne
On the warm summer day when she was born,
The longed for daughter in an all boy clan.

How her brothers loved their baby sister,
She was the apple of her family's eye.
Each would do anything to assist her
And at night would sing her a lullaby.

Then, one May night, she awoke feeling ill
And became sicker with each passing day.
When she died, people said it was God's will,
For just as God gives, so God takes away.

Women helped Martha wash her little one
And clothed the body in a cotton shroud.
After all the preparations were done,
Friends in the community were allowed

To enter the home and pay their respects.
The coffin was placed on ladderback chairs;
They sang a hymn to He who resurrects;
The funeral ended with the minister's prayers.

The coffin was then closed, the lid nailed tight
And it was covered with a black cloth pall.
She was carried to the burial site
By pallbearers as rain began to fall.

They lowered the coffin into the grave
And each one threw in a handful of sod.
The minister told them all to be brave
And know their little girl was now with God.

The Hornes returned home for a funeral meal,
Prepared for them by their neighbors and friends,
And began the time for their hearts to heal
By accepting the grief life sometimes sends.

THE FENNO HOUSE
1704

Here the widow and her daughter share
Modest, though respectable, lives.
They keep their house with well-ordered care
From which a simple beauty derives.

The kitchen on the westward side
Where crops are ground and pared for eating
Has a fireplace deep and wide
Used both for cooking and for heating.

The parlor faces to the east
Where five windows let in morning light.
So much glass the house's cost increased
But it makes the room cheerful and bright.

The west chamber with its low-post bed
Has on the floor a bearskin rug.
Here the boarder sleeps 'neath quilted spread
After the bed warmer gets him snug.

With a fenced-in garden in the back,
A few animals in the barn,
There is little these ladies lack
As they spin their wool into yarn.

The Fenno House

THE FITCH HOUSE
1737

The children in this house are doubly blest:
Their father's well-to-do, their mother is kind.
Food is abundant, they're always well-dressed.
Their conduct is constantly being refined
By many hours of parental teaching,
So they always try their best not to speak
Nor to squirm when the minister's preaching,
But that's hard to keep in mind every week.
Each day the children have many chores to do:
Churning butter, bringing in wood, snapping beans,
Weeding the garden before the day is through,
Learning all the while what a good habit means.
But when all such work is, for the moment, done,
Games, toys and stories are all the more fun.

The Fitch House

THE THOMPSON BANK
1835

With portico, columns and parapet
The bank looks like a Greek temple set
Down in the New England countryside.
People come to its doors from far and wide
For granite and iron do much to assure
All customers that their money's secure.
The white ceiling and walls of light gray
Greet those who enter on a working-day
To make a deposit or a withdrawal
At the teller's counter by the side wall.
The Argand chandelier burns whale oil
So on cloudy days the clerk can still toil
At writing letters and reviewing loans
And checking all assets that the bank owns.
If work is threatened by a winter storm
The wood stove is used to keep people warm,
For bank work can't stop, there's too much to be done
In these final years of the Age of Homespun.

The Thompson Bank

THE PRINTING OFFICE
C. 1780

Scents of linseed oil and rosin permeate
The air while men set type and run the press
As two women sew pages with finesse,
All working at an industrious rate.
A young man just starting out sweeps the floor
And cleans the type so there won't be a mess;
He runs all errands so as to impress
The master printer to teach him more
About the art and mystery of the trade.
Over the years, with hard work, he'll progress
Until at age twenty one he'll possess
The skills for which a journeyman is paid
The daily wage of a dollar fifty,
A good start in life if he is thrifty.

THE CIDER MILL
C. 1835

When leaves first begin to turn red and gold
And the morning air gets bracing and clear,
Salem Towne announces to his household
That the time to harvest apples is near.
Apples are carried by basket and cart
From the orchard to the nearby mill
And everyone in the family takes part.
For children, work is less labor than thrill
As they watch the horse-powered crushers crush
The apples to release their pungent scent
And convert the red rounded shapes to mush.
The juice is put into barrels to ferment
Into cider for a Thanksgiving toast
At the dinner Salem Towne plans to host.

THE SALEM TOWNE HOUSE
1796

Salem Towne bids us, "Enter in
Before winter's cold numbs your skin;
Come sit by the fire."

In the parlor we take a seat
And thank him for the added heat
When he piles logs higher.

His daughter serves us tea and cake,
He tells us how she loves to bake
When company's calling.

We catch up on the latest news
And pleasantly exchange our views
As the snow starts falling.

He asks with an inviting smile,
If perhaps we could stay awhile
As he completes some chores.

He tells us, "Make yourselves at home,
Mercy will, if you'd like to roam,
Show you around the floors."

So with Mercy Towne as our guide,
We take a tour of the inside
Of their wonderful rooms

Filled with ornamental looking glass,
Dresser shelves with pewter and brass,
Mahogany heirlooms,

Horsehair upholstered shield-back chairs,
Hanging glass lamp to light the stairs,
Staffordshire figurines,

Exquisite Simon Willard clocks,
Preserves stored well in jars and crocks,
Queensware jugs and tureens.

We thank Mercy Towne for her time;
We hear the grandfather clock chime,
She says, "Please stay and dine."

After dinner the snow is deep,
They both bid us to stay and sleep;
We're in bed before nine.

The Salem Towne House and Village Common

THE SALEM TOWNE GARDEN

Salem Towne Senior and son often stroll
Through their gardens in the soft evening air.
They both will tell you it's good for the soul
So they make this shared time a daily goal.

The old Brigadier-General and his heir
Discuss some experiments with fruit trees:
Their varieties of apple and pear
Have proven successful beyond compare.

They sit in the arbor and watch the bees
Among the lavender, foxglove and rose
While the hyssop sways in the gentle breeze.
"Lovely," the father says. His son agrees.

They stop near the place where corn poppy grows
To admire how they've been placed in rows.
"Do any exceed the beauty of those?"
"Of them all, they're my favorites, I suppose."

THE BULLARD TAVERN

When a stagecoach comes down the bumpy road,
Filled with passengers, hungry and weary,
It stops at a friendly wayside abode:
The Bullard tavern, a warm and cheery
Place where one will find refreshment and rest
With a bed, good food and a glass of flip.
This night the village has a special guest:
Nathaniel Hawthorne is taking a trip
 And has stopped at the tavern for the night.
He has just completed his evening meal,
When, much to his and the tavern's delight,
A showman presents, with wonderful zeal,
A diorama of England and France.
When he peers through a glass window he views
Cathedrals and castles move by in a glance.
While Nathaniel catches up on the news
People gather to watch an artist draw
A portrait of the tavern keeper's wife.
He renders her likeness without a flaw,
Commissions are better when there's no strife.
Soon, men in the taproom begin a song
By the name of "The Deceitful Young Man".
For a short time, Nathaniel sings along,
But early to bed is part of his plan,
And so, with "God speed" and "Good evening" said,
Nathaniel Hawthorne goes upstairs to bed.

THE TIN SHOP
C. 1800-1850

Here, in his small shop, the tinsmith makes
Utensils of wide variety.
His tin kitchen both roasts and bakes;
He fashions pots for coffee and tea.
Milk pans come in various sizes
As do kettles in six quarts or ten.
By the hearth, a wife utilizes
Tin measures, scoops and ladles. And when,
In winter, daylight ends close to four
And a husband's chores aren't yet complete,
The japanned lantern by the barn door
Gives needed light and a bit of heat.
Colander, skimmer, dipper and pail
All are at Asa Knight's store for sale
Or when a peddler comes down the road
Bringing his wares by the wagonload.

THE PARSONAGE
1748

The parsonage has a saltbox design:
Flat in the front with a long sloping rear.
Because the village common's so near,
A white picket fence keeps out geese and swine.

The windows contain some amethyst panes
That give a strange hue to the world outside.
The front doorway shows how the builder's pride
Prompted him to take a few extra pains

By placing dentilling over the door
And pilasters to the left and the right.
The clapboard exterior is painted white
To match Greek structures of ancient lore.

The minister's taken a room downstairs
As a place to write his sermons and speak
With the callers who see him during the week,
And when it's quiet, as a place for prayers.

A minister's family has much to do
Taking care of church business everyday.
But doing so much for so little pay,
To make ends meet, they keep a garden too.

THE JOHN MCCLELLAN LAW OFFICE
1796

John McClellan, attorney at law,
Has an office on the village green.
In the course of a day, he will draw
Up a mortgage or perhaps a lien.

This modest building is all he needs
For a place to do the legal work
Of contracts, leases, property deeds
And collecting debts from those who shirk.

His office is simple, plain and neat
With law books arranged in well kept rows.
Inside shutters help regulate heat
For comfort when writing legal prose.

Being a lawyer of some renown,
He has students, who've shown they're able,
Learn about law by writing down
Copies of writs at his worktable.

Though always greeted with much respect,
John McClellan is not a rich man.
Known for his lawyerly intellect,
He also farms to feed his large clan.

THE ASA KNIGHT STORE
C. 1810

By the green is Asa Knight's store
From which he sells items galore.
Arabian spice
To a cast iron vise
Await those who open his door.

Some customers pay him in cash
They keep in their own private cache.
Glass, coffee and hooks
Brooms, linen and books
Are theirs when they go to their stash.

Most pay him with things they have made,
They come not with cash but a trade.
For butter and cheese
They get sugar and teas
And for enough turkeys, brocade.

When the weather turns warmer in May,
Asa goes to the city to stay
'til he sells everything
His customers bring
Then returns with more goods to display.

THE VILLAGE COMMON

The village common, sometimes called a green,
Is a patch of land located between
The Meetinghouse and home of Salem Towne,
A rectangle covered with dung and down
Deposited by a gaggle of geese
Who take it upon themselves to police
The area and keep it safe from foes.
Children know, when playing, to watch their toes
To keep them from a goose's angry beak
Or from stepping where they're sure to shriek.

THE SHOE SHOP
C. 1800-1850

In this shop, young men with quick, steady hands
Can peg three to five pairs of shoes a day.
The shoes are then sent to faraway lands
Or to local stores where people will pay
All the way up to two dollars a pair.
That might mean spending a day's pay or more,
But working all day, a man has to wear
Sturdy shoes so that his feet don't get sore.
Although shoe leather is heavy and stiff,
It will, over time, conform to the feet,
And can be preserved and protected, if
Rubbed with grease, for use in rain, snow and sleet.
The shoemaker toils at a humble trade,
But men can't work if their shoes aren't well made.

THE POUND

When sheep, cows or horses go astray
And roam into a neighbor's garden,
They're brought to the pound where they will stay
Until a fine is paid for pardon.
While they wait inside the fieldstone walls,
Built high to prevent their leaping free,
They fill the air with such raucous calls
To plead with the keeper of the key:
"We promise never again to roam,
Now please release us. Let us go home."

COUNTRYSIDE

THE DISTRICT SCHOOL
C. 1800-1810

When the harvest is safely gathered in
And stored away in cellar, loft and bin
And weather turns cold and skies threaten snow,
It's time for the Freeman children to go
To the district school until spring returns
And their father Pliny once again turns
The soil of his fields with his horse and plow.
But all that work is months away; for now
Beulah, Florella, Augusta and Dwight
Will spend their days learning to read and write.
Delia will learn her geography
While Pliny Jr. studies history.
Silas, the oldest, will sometimes assist
Should a young scholar his lessons resist.
But most are happy who go to this school
For their teacher lives by the Golden Rule,
So while she is strict she is fair and just
And children learn more from teachers they trust,
Even if their schoolroom is often dark
And the walls around them are dull and stark.

THE HERVEY BROOKS POTTERY SHOP
C. 1819

At the last light of another long day,
Hervey Brooks closes his pottery shop
After hours of making pots from clay.
At seventy years, some say he should stop
Laboring so every day of his life
And enjoy the rewards of his hard work.

"Staying home too much will trouble my wife.
Call it long habit, perhaps it's a quirk,
But nothing I do gives me more pleasure
Than fashioning inkstands, jugs, cups and pans.
My porringers and bowls are my treasure,
So, no, slowing down is not in my plans.
In spite of my age, I'm not yet tired
Of shaping lumps of clay into redware jars.
I have a kiln load set to be fired,
So one night soon, I'll mix embers with stars.
It takes a hardwood cord and three cords pine
For fire enough to bake clay and melt glaze.
The heat must be just right to call the work mine.
When I draw the kiln I always appraise
Each piece and discard what's not fit to sell,
Then pack for retail and wholesale the rest.
Folks favor my wares, so the peddlers tell,
It sells down in Georgia and even out west."

THE POWDER HOUSE

Should an enemy someday threaten harm,
New England militias will swiftly arm
And give any foe a forceful reply.
In the meantime, they keep their powder dry.

THE PLINY FREEMAN FARM
HOUSE C. 1810-1815, BARN C. 1830-50
CORN BARN C. 1830-60, SMOKEHOUSE C. 1800

Work on the Freeman farm is never done.
While their labors vary by the season,
Every month provides its own good reason
To do all chores well and overlook none,
So through the year all work from sun to sun.

Spring is the time of year for storing wood
For fireplaces and split-rail fences;
This work's begun soon after March commences.
Manuring in April is understood;
It assures that the harvest will be good.

Gardens in summer need constant weeding.
A scythe will lay the grass in even rows
If it is sharp and held by one who knows
What makes for graceful swings while proceeding.
The livestock, of course, always need feeding.

Autumn is the time for taking in maize
Along with a little wheat, flax and rye.
Apples are gathered for cider and pie
When Indian summer brings its blue haze
And the rolling year's most pleasant days.

House sills must be banked with corn stalks and leaves
Before bitter winds blow and snowflakes fall.
With plenty stored up for kitchen and stall,
Mrs. Freeman spins and her husband weaves,
Thus by the hearth do they spend winter eves.

The Pliny Freeman Farm

THE COOPER SHOP
C. 1840

In winter, the cooper cuts and hauls wood,
Splits it by hand, and stacks it up to dry
So when harvest time comes, it will be good
For making barrels customers will buy.
White oak is used for barrels of cider,
Red oak for barrels of apples and grain.
All the work of the family provider,
Without proper storage, would be in vain
Thus the cooper works hard, knowing the task
Set before him benefits his neighbor.
The skill he employs when making a cask
Reveals one who cares about his labor.
His firkins and buckets, being all well made,
Give him, when not farming, a prosperous trade.

The Cooper's Shop

THE BIXBY HOUSE
C. 1800-1810
ADDITIONS C. 1820 AND 1838-45

Emerson Bixby and Laura, his spouse,
Live with their daughters in a modest house,
But the 19th century's a time of change;
They're living a life they'd once have found strange
For commerce has brought new ways to provide
To people living in the countryside
All manner of goods once a luxury.
In this time of expanding industry,
Laura and her daughters work together
In their home sewing pieces of leather
That will be used for the upper parts of shoes
And braiding straw for hats. Emerson pursues
His work of shoeing and making repairs
But now also manufacturing wares
To meet a growing consumer demand
That is causing his business to expand.
With all their hard work, they're able to buy
New wallpapers and paints to beautify
The rooms of the house both up and downstairs
And place in the parlor a sofa and chairs.
Laura's bought printed cotton for dresses
And her new dish set always impresses
When her friends stop by for neighborly chats
Wearing the latest in factory made hats.

THE BLACKSMITH SHOP
C. 1802-10

Daily, at his forge, the blacksmith labors
At his noisy and extremely hot trade.
Many are the tools he's repaired and made,
Many are the horses shoed for his neighbors.
Children love to see him pump the bellows
And watch colors get increasingly bright
As they glow in the smithy's gloomy light,
Kept dim to discern shades of reds and yellows,
For if the fire's too hot, iron will burn
And an afternoon's work would be for naught.
This is a lesson an apprentice is taught
And, if he wants to know success, must learn.
He uses charcoal to heat and soften
Iron, then shapes it with a hammer and anvil.
As with any trade, he has gained his skill
By watching, listening, and doing, often.
During July, he puts his hammer down
And joins the other men to bring in hay.
While he does this partly for the good pay,
He changes work for the sake of his town.

THE DUMMERSTON BRIDGE

A covered bridge spans the village pond
So folks can get to the mills and beyond.
It's covered to protect it from the weather;
How long a bridge lasts depends on whether
Its underpinnings are sheltered by a roof:
A bridge might stand 80 years if weather-proof.
The bridge's designer is Ithiel Town,
An architect of no little renown.
His truss design is cheap and easy to build,
Even if workers are somewhat unskilled
They can be taught to use lumber at hand
To build a structure that, although not grand,
Does well the job for which it's intended:
To provide a way. For this, it's splendid.

The Dummerston Bridge

47
SPRUNG FROM THE SOIL

48
SPRUNG FROM THE SOIL

MILL NEIGHBORHOOD

THE CARDING MILL
C. 1840

Oliver Hapgood's wonderful machine
Can produce rolls of wool in one hour;
It uses a small stream for power.
Wool is fed into it, tangled but clean,

From a conveyer belt called a feed apron
Where licker-ins take wool to the tumbler
Which deposits it on the main cylinder.
This carries it along through the machine, then

It is removed by workers and taken back
To the cylinder by strippers until near
The end where a fancy fluffs the wool. Here
A doffer will remove it from the track

And it's rolled up for spinning as it passes
between fluted cylinder and concave shell.
Carding mills served their communities well
Until factories made cloth for the masses.

THE GRIST MILL
BUILT BY OSV, 1938

For quite some time, snow and ice
Locked the wheel in a frozen vise,
But now, again, the water flows
And to the mill the housewife goes.
She brings with her a sack of wheat
Which her hungry family will eat
After it's been ground for flour.
She comes at an early hour
To have all day for baking bread
That her family may be well fed.
After the miller takes his toll,
He pours the grain into a hole
In the upper, or runner, stone.
He opens the sluice; with a groan
The runner wheel begins to spin
Above its lower bed stone twin.
Not quite touching, the runner moves
Over the bed stone. Both have grooves
That, like scissor blades, cut the grain.
A chest stands ready to contain,
As it moves off the stones, the grist
Which the miller, as his sons assist,
Scoops into the customer's sack,
Then to her home she hurries back.

The Grist Mill

THE SAW MILL
REPRODUCED BY OSV, 1984

When spring comes 'round, the streams and rivers flow
With fast moving water from melted snow,
Thus giving sawyers the power they need
For making their work of sawing succeed.
Pliny Freeman's oxen haul logs to the mill;
He pays by the board foot when given the bill.
His sons, of course, assist him with this task.
He explains how the mill works when they ask.
"The water coming down the flume will turn
The reaction wheel fastened within the cistern.
The wheel, through a crank, and an arm called the sweep,
Connects to the sash or gate. The sash will keep
The blade strung tight as it saws through the wood.
By the end of the day, the sawyer should
Cut as much lumber as we could in a week."
Just then, his oldest son begins to speak.
"Father, I see some power from the gate
Is used to turn a large gear and create
The means to move the carriage on which logs rest.
This causes the log to always be pressed
Up good and tight as it's pulled through the blade
And cut on the downstroke, thus boards are made!"
"That large gear you mention is called a rag wheel.
Now, let's return home for our noonday meal.
We'll finish some chores and then we'll come back.
I doubt it will take us much time to stack
The boards in the wagon, you're all getting strong,
You'll be doing a man's work before too long.
Tomorrow, I'll teach you how hammer and nail
Can build a shed able to withstand a gale."

The Saw Mill

57
SPRUNG FROM THE SOIL

Made in the USA
Coppell, TX
06 December 2020